Dad Jokes
Book Bonanza

Dad Jokes Book Bonanza

615 Whoppers of Laughter, Groans, and Good Times.
Your Ultimate Source of Family Fun!

Mauricio Vasquez
Toronto, Canada

Dad Jokes Book Bonanza by Aria Capri Publishing Group [Aria Capri International Inc.].
All Rights Reserved.

Authors:
Mauricio Vasquez

First Printing: January 2024
ISBN-978-1-990709-94-4

Introduction

Welcome to a laughter-filled journey! "Dad Jokes Book Bonanza: 615 Whoppers of Laughter, Groans, and Good Times" is your gateway to mastering the art of dad jokes – those wonderfully corny quips that make you groan and giggle in equal measure.

In these pages lies a treasure trove of humor, spanning 62 diverse categories. We've got jokes to lighten every moment, from the trials of parenting to the nuances of office life. This book isn't just a collection of jokes; it's a celebration of simple, heartfelt humor that transcends ages and trends.

But there's more! Dive into our special section, "Mastering the Art of Dad Jokes," where you'll learn the craft behind the laughter. Discover the timing, the delivery, and the secret sauce that makes dad jokes a beloved art form. Whether you're the family comedian or just looking to spice up your humor game, this guide is your compass.

Dad jokes are about connecting, sharing joy, and turning the ordinary into memorable moments. They prove that humor doesn't need to be complex to be cherished.

So, as you explore "Dad Jokes Book Bonanza," let go of your inhibitions. Embrace the cheesy, the punny, and the downright silly. Get ready to laugh, groan, and roll your eyes. The delightful world of dad jokes awaits!

Spread the Cheer: Your Quick Review Guide!

Loved "Dad Jokes Book Bonanza"? Share the joy! A quick, witty review can be your way of passing the laughter baton.

If our jokes had you chuckling or even groaning in delight, consider leaving a five-star review. It's like giving a high-five to dad humor! Your feedback helps more people discover the magic of simple, hearty laughs.

So, grab those stars, pen a line or two, and help keep the dad joke legacy alive! 📖 ✴ 😄

To leave your review, please scan this QR code. Thank you!

Table of Contents

Amazon 13

Alcohol 14

Art 15

Artificial Intelligence 16

Babies 18

Beer 19

Being sick 20

Birthdays 22

Books 23

Bosses 24

Camping 26

Cars 27

Christmas 28

Computers 30

Dads 31

Dating 33

Daughters 34

Death 36

Doctors 37

Driving 39

.... 40

Entrepreneurship 40

Farts 41

Fathers-in-Law 43

Food 45

Getting old 46

Grilling 47

Golf 49

Grandparents 50

Houses 54

Inflation 56

Insurance 57

Internet 58

Lawyers 60

Leaving a job 61

Life 62

Love 64

Marriage 65

Moms 67

Mothers-in-Law 71

Newborns 73

Pets 77

Retirement 78

School 79

Sports 83

Summer 84

Technology 85

Transit 87

Trucks 88

Time 89

Underwear 91

Winter 92

Wives 93

Work 95

Workouts 96

Zombies 97

Amazon

1. Q: Why did the book join Amazon?

   A: It wanted to be best-seller.

2. Q: What do you call an Amazon Echo that tells dad jokes?

   A: A dad-a-base.

3. Q: Why did the Amazon package go to therapy?

   A: It had too much baggage.

4. Q: What did the Amazon River say to the rainforest?

   A: "I stream through your area."

5. Q: Why don't Amazon warriors play cards?

   A: They hate dealing with defeat.

6. Q: Why did the parrot order a mirror from Amazon?

   A: It wanted to talk to itself.

7. Q: What did the cat order on Amazon?

   A: A box. Just the box.

8. Q: Why did the banana go to Amazon?

   A: It wanted to update its peel.

9. Q: Why did the Amazon package look sad?

A: It missed its prime.

10. Q: Why did the Amazon delivery guy become a gardener?

A: He was good at leaving packages in the bush.

Alcohol

11. Q: I told my wife I was going to make a bike out of wine bottles.

A: She said, "You can't be sirius."

12. Q: Why did the grape stop in the middle of the road?

A: Because he ran out of wine.

13. Q: What do you call a group of alcoholic ghosts?

A: Spirits.

14. Q: Why don't alcoholics play hide and seek?

A: Because good luck hiding when you're lit!

15. I told my kids I'd read them a book about anti-gravity.

They were so excited, they couldn't put it down!

16. **Q: Why did the tomato turn red?**

    A: Because it saw the salad dressing with vodka.

17. **Q: What did the bartender say after Charles Dickens ordered a martini?**

    A: "Olive or twist?"

18. **I tried to write a joke about ethanol,** but it's not all it's cracked up to beer.

19. **Q: Why was the math book sad at the bar?**

    A: Because it had too many problems on tap

Art

20. **Q: Why did Van Gogh become a painter?**

    A: Because he didn't have an ear for music.

21. **Q: Why did the artist go to jail?**

    A: Because he had a brush with the law.

22. **Q: What do you call an artistic fish?**

    A: A drawfish.

23. **Q: Why was the belt sent to art school?**

A: For holding up the pants beautifully.

24. **Q: Why did the painting go to school?**

A: It needed to learn more about art history.

25. **Q: Why did the sculpture break up with the painting?**

A: It said their relationship was too surface-level.

26. **Q: What did the canvas say to the paintbrush?**

A: "I'm drawn to you."

27. **Q: Why did the artist break up with his girlfriend?**

A: Because he didn't like her tone.

28. **Q: Why don't art thieves feel remorse?**

A: They don't have any con-science.

29. **Q: What do you call an artistic pumpkin?**

A: A Jack-of-all-arts

Artificial Intelligence

30. **Q: Why was the robot so bad at soccer?**

A: Because it had a metal breakdown.

31. Q: Why don't robots have brothers?

A: Because they only have transistors.

32. Q: What do you call an artistic robot?

A: A draw-bot.

33. Q: Why was the computer cold?

A: It left its Windows open.

34. Q: Why did the AI go to school?

A: To improve its learning algorithm.

35. Q: Why don't robots get scared?

A: Because they have nerves of steel.

36. Q: What did the robot say to the centipede?

A: "Stop being so leggy!"

37. Q: Why was the AI bad at telling jokes?

A: It always missed the punchline.

38. Q: Why did the robot go on a diet?

A: It had too many bytes.

39. Q: Why don't robots ever panic?

A: Because they always keep their cool-ant.

Babies

40. Q: Why was the baby strawberry crying?

A: Because its parents were in a jam.

41. Q: Why don't babies play hide and seek?

A: Because they always wail when they're found.

42. Q: What do you call a group of baby soldiers?

A: Infantry.

43. Q: Why was the baby computer so smart?

A: It had a byte-sized brain.

44. Q: Why don't babies write tests?

A: They always drool on the answer sheet.

45. Q: Why did the baby go to the doctor?

A: Because it had a bad case of the rattles.

46. Q: Why did the baby corn ask the mama corn?

A: "Where's popcorn?"

47. Q: Why was the baby cookie sad?

A: Because its mom was a wafer too long.

48. Q: What did the baby volcano say to its mom?

A: "I lava you!"

49. Q: Why was the baby ant confused?

A: Because all his uncles were ants.

Beer

50. Q: Why don't beers ever get into arguments?

A: They always prefer to be ale-mates.

51. Q: What do you call a bear that loves beer?

A: A brewin'.

52. Q: Why did the beer file a police report?

A: It got mugged.

53. Q: How do you know a beer is optimistic?

A: It always looks at the glass as half full.

54. Q: What's a beer's favorite book?

A: "The Great Gats-beer."

55. Q: Why don't beers work as librarians?

A: They're always getting checked out.

56. Q: What's a beer's life philosophy?

A: "Ale's well that ends well."

57. Q: Why did the beer go to the party?

A: It wanted to be the toast of the town.

58. Q: Why did the beer break up with the water?

A: It said, "You're just too bland for me."

59. Q: What's a beer's favorite type of joke?

A: Pint-sized puns!

Being sick

60. Q: Why don't sick people tell secrets?

A: Because they always cough it up.

61. Q: What did the sick lemon say to the lime?

A: "Give me some space, I'm feeling a little sour."

62. **Q: Why was the computer cold?**

   A: It caught a virus.

63. **Q:Why don't sick jokes get told in hospitals?**

   A: They don't want to spread.

64. **Q: Why did the germ cross the microscope?**

   A: To get to the other slide.

65. **Q: What do you call a sick eagle?**

   A: Illegal.

66. **Q: Why did the tissue dance?**

   A: Because it had a little boogie in it.

67. **Q: Why don't sick people play cards?**

   A: Because they might deal with a virus.

68. **Q: What did one tonsil say to the other tonsil?**

   A: "Get dressed, the doctor is taking us out!"

69. **Q: Why was the computer sneezing?**

   A: It had a bad case of "digital flu."

70.   Q: Why are birthday balloons so wise?

     A: Because they're filled with helium.

71.   Q: What did the tiger say to her cub on his birthday?

     A: "You're roar-some!"

72.   Q: Why did the birthday cake visit the psychologist?

     A: Because it felt crumby.

73.   Q: What does a clam do on its birthday?

     A: It shell-ebrates!

74.   Q: Why did the birthday card go to school?

     A: It wanted to be well-writ-ten.

75.   Q: What kind of birthday cake do ghosts prefer?

     A: I scream cake!

76.   Q: Why was the birthday candle feeling so zen?

     A: It found inner peas.

77.   Q: What did the birthday balloon say to the pin?

     A: "You're point-ful."

78. **Q: How do pickles celebrate their birthday?**

A: They relish the moment.

79. **Q: Why don't birthdays play hide and seek?**

A: Because they always end up in a party!

Books

80. **Q: Why don't books have friends?**

A: Because they always shut people out.

81. **I read a book about anti-gravity.** *It was impossible to put down.*

82. **Q: Why was the book always in trouble?**

A: It never could keep its cover.

83. **Q: What do you call a dinosaur that loves reading?**

A: A Thesaurus.

84. **Q: Why don't books like to play hide and seek?**

A: Because they're always spotted.

85. I read a book about the history of glue – can't put it down.

86. Q: Why did the librarian get kicked off the plane?

A: Because it was overbooked.

87. Q: Why don't books join the army?

A: Because they hate the draft.

88. I'm reading a book on the history of erasers. It's not bad, but it has no real ending.

89. Q: Why did the book join the police?

A: It wanted to go undercover.

Bosses

90. Q: Why did the boss bring a ladder to work?

A: He wanted to get to the top.

91. Q: What did the boss say to the light bulb?

A: "You're really bright!"

92. Q: Why did the boss go to art class?

A: To brush up on his skills.

93. **Q: What do you call a boss at the beach?**

    A: Sandy.

94. **Q: Why was the computer cold at work?**

    A: The boss left his Windows open.

95. **Q: Why did the boss bring a clock to the meeting?**

    A: To make up for lost time.

96. **Q: What did the boss say to the employee?**

    A: "You're the highlight of my day."

97. **Q: Why did the boss hire a kangaroo?**

    A: Because he wanted someone who was great at jumping through hoops.

98. **Q: What did the boss say to the employee who built a time machine?**

    A: "Great, now you can meet all your deadlines yesterday!"

99. **Q: Why was the boss so good at gardening?**

    A: He was great at growing the business.

Camping

100. Q: Why don't some people like camping?

   A: It's just too in-tents.

101. Q: Why did the camping trip become a musical?

   A: Because of all the pitches.

102. Q: What's a tree's favorite camping snack?

   A: S'more leaves, please.

103. Q: Why don't campfires share their stories?

   A: They're afraid they might spread.

104. Q: Why did the tent break up with the sleeping bag?

   A: It was too clingy.

105. Q: What do you call a bear with no teeth?

   A: A gummy bear... especially around campfires.

106. Q: Why did the campfire look so bright?

   A: It was lit.

107. Q: How do you start a camping party?

A: You pitch a tent.

108. Q: Why did the camper bring string to the campsite?

A: To tie up loose ends.

109. Q: Why did the marshmallow go camping?

A: It wanted to become a toasted marshmallow.

Cars

110. Q: Why did the car apply for a job?

A: It wanted to shift gears in life.

111. Q: What do you call a laughing motorcycle?

A: A Yamahahaha

112. Q: Why did the old car hate new music?

A: It only played the classics.

113. Q: Why did the car go to school?

A: Because it wanted to improve its driving skills.

114. Q: What do you call a country where everyone drives a red car?

A: A red carnation.

115. **Q: Why was the car always tired?**

    A: It had too many exhausted pipes.

116. **Q: What did the electric car say during a thunderstorm?**

    A: "This weather is shocking!"

117. **Q: Why don't cars get cold in the winter?**

    A: They come with built-in heaters.

118. **Q: What do you call a car that tells jokes?**

    A: A car-median.

119. **Q: Why did the car get a trophy?**

    A: It had outstanding performance.

Christmas

120. **Q: What do you get if you cross Santa with a duck?**

    A: A Christmas Quacker.

121. **Q: Why was Santa's little helper feeling depressed?**

A: He had low "elf" esteem.

122. Q: **What do you call a broke Santa?**

A: Saint Nickel-less.

123. Q: **What's Santa's favorite type of music?**

A: Wrap.

124. Q: **Why did Santa go to school?**

A: To improve his "elf"-ucation.

125. Q: **Why was the Christmas tree bad at knitting?**

A: It kept dropping its needles.

126. Q: **What do snowmen eat for breakfast?**

A: Frosted Flakes.

127. Q: **What did one snowman say to the other?**

A: "Do you smell carrots?"

128. Q: **Why don't Christmas trees knit?**

A: They always drop their needles.

129. Q: **What did the gingerbread man put on his bed?**

A: A cookie sheet.

Computers

130. Q: Why was the computer cold?

    A: It left its Windows open.

131. Q: Why don't computers like to play hide and seek?

    A: Because they always get found by the cursor.

132. Q: What do you call a singing laptop?

    A: A Dell.

133. Q: Why was the computer so smart?

    A: Because it had a hard drive.

134. Q: Why did the computer break up with the internet?

    A: There was no connection.

135. Q: Why do programmers love nature?

    A: Because it has so many loops.

136. Q: What's a computer's favorite snack?

    A: Microchips.

137. Q: Why don't computers go to school?

A: Because they have too many bytes of knowledge.

138. Q: Why did the computer go to the doctor?

A: It had a virus.

139. Q: Why was the computer so good at golf?

A: Because it had a hard drive.

Dads

140. Q: Why did the dad stare at the can of orange juice for hours?

A: Because it said, "Concentrate." Man, you ever notice how dads take things way too literally?

141. Q: What do you call a dad who's excellent at yoga?

A: The "Bend-master." You know, because every time he tries to bend down, something cracks!

142. **Q: What did the dad say about his new job as an elevator operator?**

A: "It has its ups and downs, but I'm elevating my career!"

Classic dad, always elevating the pun game.

143. **Q: What do you call a dad who falls through the ice?**

A: A pop-sicle!

144. **Q: Why did the dad sit on the clock?**

A: He wanted to be on time.

145. **Q: What did the dad say about his soup?**

A: "This is souperb!"

146. **Q: Why don't dads trust atoms?**

A: Because they make up everything.

147. **Q: How do dads follow Will Smith in the snow?**

A: They follow the fresh prints.

148. **Q: Why did the dad take a job at the bakery?**

A: Because he kneaded dough.

149. **Q: What do you call a dad who's a furniture designer?**

A: A chair-man.

Dating

150. Q: Why don't oysters go on dates?

A: They're shellfish.

151. Q: What did the pickle say to the date?

A: "You mean a great dill to me."

152. Q: Why don't programmers go on dates?

A: They can't escape their loops.

153. Q: What did the ghost say to his date?

A: "You look boo-tiful tonight."

154. Q: Why did the date at the restaurant go well?

A: Because they had great chemistry, and the food was sodium good.

155. Q: What did the magnet say to its date?

A: "I find you very attractive."

156. Q: Why don't cats use dating apps?

A: They prefer a more purr-sonal connection.

157. **Q: Why was the calendar the best at dating?**

    A: It always had a date.

158. **Q: What did the drum say to its date?**

    A: "You've got me beat."

159. **Q: Why was the football player a bad date?**

    A: He kept passing the time.

Daughters

160. **Q: What did the dad say to his daughter before her soccer game?**

    A: "I hope you score a goal, but remember, it's not the end of the world if you don't."

161. **Q: Why did the dad teach his daughter to be good at math?**

    A: So she'd always count on herself.

162. Q: What did the father buffalo say to his daughter when she left for college?

A: "Bison."

163. Q: Why did the daughter eat her homework?

A: Because her dad said it was a piece of cake.

164. Q: What did the dad say to his daughter who wanted to sleep in a tree?

A: "It's not a good idea, you might fall out and branch your arm."

165. Q: Why did the dad always joke about the moon?

A: To teach his daughter it's okay to shoot for the stars.

166. Q: Why did the dad tell his daughter to be like a math problem?

A: So she'd always be a challenge to solve.

167. Q: What did the dad name his daughter who loved to watch the stars?

A: Stella.

168. **Q: Why did the dad buy his daughter a trampoline?**

A: So she could always bounce back from setbacks.

169. **Q: Why did the dad tell his daughter jokes every night?**

A: To ensure her dreams were filled with laughter.

Death

170. **Q: Why don't some people want to write their will?**

A: They're afraid it's a dead giveaway.

171. **Q: What do you call a dead parrot?**

A: Polygon.

172. **Q: Why was the cemetery so popular?**

A: People were dying to get in.

173. **Q: Why don't ghosts like rain?**

A: It dampens their spirits.

174. **Q: What did one casket say to the other casket?**

A: "Is that you coffin?"

175. **Q: Why don't skeletons fight each other?**

   A: They don't have the guts.

176. **Q: Why was the gravestone so tired?**

   A: It was dead on its feet.

177. **Q: What do you call a cleaning skeleton?**

   A: The grim sweeper.

178. **Q: Why don't mummies take time off?**

   A: They're afraid to unwind.

179. **Q: Why did the skeleton go to the party alone?**

   A: Because he had no body to go with him. Classic

skeleton, always rattling around solo.

Doctors

180. **Q: Why did the doctor carry a red pen?**

   A: In case they needed to draw blood.

181. **Q: What did the doctor say to the rocket ship?**

   A: "Time to get your booster shot."

182. Q: Why did the doctor start painting?

A: He wanted to have a more colorful patient palette.

183. Q: What do you call an angry doctor?

A: An ill-tempered doctor.

184. Q: Why was the doctor always calm?

A: Because he had a lot of patients.

185. Q: What did the doctor say to the sick computer?

A: "It looks like you've got a virus!"

186. Q: Why did the doctor carry a stethoscope?

A: To listen to the heartbeat of the problem.

187. Q: What did the doctor say to the clock?

A: "Your time is ticking perfectly."

188. Q: Why did the doctor become a gardener?

A: He had a green thumb for healing.

189. Q: What did the doctor say to the sick joke book?

A: "You need a good laugh."

Driving

190. Q: Why don't cars play soccer?

    A: Because they're afraid of getting a red card.

191. Q: What did the traffic light say to the car?

    A: "Don't look, I'm changing!"

192. Q: Why did the tomato turn red while driving?

    A: Because it saw the salad dressing at the stoplight.

193. Q: Why don't ghosts like to drive?

    A: They can't handle the steering wheel.

194. Q: What do you call a sleeping car?

    A: A car-nap.

195. Q: What do you call a group of musical car tires?

    A: A rubber band. They've got some real traction in the music industry.

196. Q: What do you call a singing car?

    A: A car-aoke machine.

197.   Q: Why did the wheel refuse to play cards with the other car parts?

A: It was tired of spinning around in circles. Talk about a wheel with an attitude.

198.   Q: Why did the computer crash while driving?

A: It had a bad driver.

199.   Q: What did one traffic light say to the other?

A: "Stop looking, I'm changing!"

Entrepreneurship

200.   Q: Why did the entrepreneur become a gardener?

A: To grow his business.

201.   Q: What did the entrepreneurial lemon say?

A: "When life gives you lemons, make a startup."

202.   Q: Why don't entrepreneurs tell jokes timing?

A: They're always working on their punch line.

203.   Q: What do you call an entrepreneur in a bakery?

A: A dough-maker.

204. Q: **Why did the entrepreneur open a bakery?**

A: He wanted to make some dough.

205. Q: **What did the computer do at its startup?**

A: It had a few bytes.

206. Q: **Why did the calendar start a business?**

A: It had a lot of dates.

207. Q: **What did the entrepreneurial fish say?**

A: "I'm starting a new stream of income."

208. Q: **Why did the entrepreneur become a pirate?**

A: To increase his net worth.

209. Q: **Why don't spiders become entrepreneurs?**

A: They don't like to leave their web.

Farts

210. Q: **Why don't scientists trust farts?**

A: They can't always hold their gas.

211. Q: Why was the fart so proud?

A: Because it thought it was a blast.

212. Q: What do you call a ghost fart?

A: A spirit toot.

213. Q: Why did the fart go to therapy?

A: It had too much internal conflict.

214. Q: What's a fart's favorite type of music?

A: Be-bop.

215. Q: Why did the fart lose the race?

A: It ran out of gas.

216. Q: Why don't farts do well in school?

A: They always get expelled.

217. Q: What do you call a secret fart?

A: A private tutor.

218. Q: Why did the fart go to the party?

A: To raise a stink.

219. Q: Why was the fart so popular?

A: Because it was always cutting up.

Fathers-in-Law

220. Q: Why do fathers-in-law avoid looking at their watches?

A: They don't want to be reminded that time is ticking with their daughter's choice.

221. Q: What do you call a father-in-law who's a great fisherman?

A: A reel-in-law.

222. Q: Why did the father-in-law go to the bank?

A: To keep his cents in the family.

223. Q: How many fathers-in-law does it take to change a light bulb?

A: Just one, but he'll make sure you know how he used to do it.

224. **Q: Why don't fathers-in-law ever get lost?**

   A: They never take directions from anyone else.

225. **Q: What's a father-in-law's favorite game to play?**

   A: "Who's the Boss?" - He always wins.

226. **Q: Why did the father-in-law sit on the TV remote?**

   A: Because he wanted to control the situation.

227. **Q: What do you call a father-in-law with a hammer?**

   A: The judge and jury.

228. **Q: Why did the father-in-law bring a ladder to our house?**

   A: To show that he's always a step above.

229. **Q: Why are fathers-in-law like coffee?**

   A: The best ones are rich, warm, and can keep you up all night with their stories.

Food

230. Q: Why don't eggs tell jokes?

    A: They might crack up.

231. Q: What do you call cheese that isn't yours?

    A: Nacho cheese.

232. Q: Why was the tomato blushing?

    A: Because it saw the salad dressing.

233. Q: What do you call a fake noodle?

    A: An impasta.

234. Q: Why did the scarecrow become a successful chef?

    A: He was outstanding in his field.

235. Q: What do you call a sleeping pizza?

    A: A piZZZZa.

236. Q: Why don't some couples go to the restaurant anymore?

    A: Because they lost their appetite for destruction.

237. Q: How does a hamburger introduce its girlfriend?

A: Meet Patty!

238. Q: Why was the cookie sad?

A: Because its mom was a wafer so long.

239. Q: What did the grape do when it got stepped on?

A: It let out a little wine.

Getting old

240. Q: Why don't old people play hide and seek?

A: Because they always forget where to hide.

241. Q: Why did the old man put his money in the blender?

A: He wanted to make liquid assets.

242. Q: What did the old phone say?

A: "At my age, I've seen a ring or two."

243. Q: Why did the old man go to the art gallery?

A: To get a little culture in his old age.

244. Q: What did the old man say about playing hide and seek?

A: "I would play, but by the time I count to ten, I forget what I'm doing!"

245. Q: What did the old man say about his bad knee?

A. "It's not what it used to be."

246. Q: Why did the old clock stop working?

A: It couldn't keep up with the times.

247. Q: What do you call an old snowman?

A: Water.

248. Q: Why did the old man become a baker?

A: To make some dough in his retirement.

249. Q: Why did the old man put a clock under his desk?

A: To work overtime.

Grilling

250. Q: Why did the dad stay by the grill?

A: He couldn't take the heat out of the kitchen.

251. Q: What did the steak say on the grill?

A: "I'm sizzling hot!"

252. Q: Why did the dad bring a tool to the barbecue?

A: He wanted to hammer out the details.

253. Q: What do you call a dad who's a master of the grill?

A: The Grill Sergeant.

254. Q: Why did the sausage quit grilling?

A: It was too burnt out.

255. Q: What did the dad say about grilling vegetables?

A: "Lettuce grill!"

256. Q: Why don't vegetables complain on the grill?

A: They relish the heat.

257. Q: Why did the dad talk to his grill?

A: He liked a little BBQ and A.

258. Q: What do you call a grilled cheese made by a dad?

A: Grate.

259. Q: Why was the grill so smart?

A: It had a lot of hot ideas.

Golf

260. **Q: Why did the golfer bring two pairs of pants?**

   A: In case he got a hole in one.

261. **Q: What did the golf ball say to the club?**

   A: "Please, don't hit me again!"

262. **Q: Why did the golfer wear two watches?**

   A: Because he had too much time on his hands and not enough holes!

263. **Q: Why are golfers good at solving puzzles?**

   A: They're not afraid of the rough.

264. **Q: What do you call a golfer who loses all of his balls?**

   A: A lost cause.

265. **Q: Why did the golfer bring a ladder to the course?**

   A: He heard about the high stakes and wanted to raise his game.

266. **Q: Why was Cinderella so bad at golf?**

A: She kept running away from the ball.

267. Q: What do you call a golfer with bad eyesight?

A: A fore-eyed monster.

268. Q: Why don't golfers ever hide their feelings?

A: Because you can always see their true swings.

269. Q: Why was the golf team so bad at math?

A: They couldn't find the right angle.

Grandparents

270. Q: Why don't grandparents use bookmarks?

A: They prefer to rely on their memory.

271. Q: What do you call grandparents who can jump higher than a house?

A: Super-elastic!

272. Q: Why did the grandparent take up gardening?

A: To grow old gracefully.

273. Q: How do grandparents write to each other?

A: In cursive, because they're classy.

274. Q: **Why are grandparents so good at chess?**

A: They've got the most experience moving the pieces.

275. Q: **What did the grandparent say about their old knees?**

A: "They're past their prime."

276. Q: **Why did the grandparent sit in the rocking chair with a ruler?**

A: To measure how long they napped.

277. Q: **How do grandparents keep their stories so interesting?**

A: They've got a lifetime of plot twists.

278. Q: **Why did the grandparent refuse to watch silent films?**

A: They liked to hear a good story.

279. Q: **Why are grandparents like stars?**

A: They're always shining down on us.

280. Q: Why don't budgets have fun?

A: They're too constrained.

281. Q: What did the budget say to the paycheck?

A: "You make my day balance."

282. Q: Why did the money go to school?

A: To improve its cents.

283. Q: What do you call a broke budget?

A: A zero-sum game.

284. Q: Why was the budget so confusing?

A: It didn't make any cents.

285. Q: What did the budget say to the expensive purchase?

A: "You're not in my league."

286. Q: Why did the budget go to the gym?

A: To trim the fat.

287. Q: What do you call a tight budget?

A: A thin wallet.

288. Q: Why was the budget so sad?

A: It was a little short.

289. Q: Why don't budgets like vacations?

A: They can't account for them.

Hospitals

290. Q: Why did the hospital get bad ratings?

A: It had no patients.

291. Q: What did the sick floor say to the hospital?

A: "I'm feeling under the weather."

292. Q: Why don't hospitals play hide and seek?

A: Because they always end up in ER.

293. Q: What did the hospital say to the ambulance?

A: "You're wheely fast!"

294. Q: Why did the hospital become an artist?

A: It had a lot of patients to draw from.

295. Q: What do you call a hospital that's on fire?

A: An inflamed-ary.

296. Q: Why did the computer go to the hospital?

A: It had a virus.

297. Q: What did the thermometer say to the sick hospital?

A: "You've got a temperature."

298. Q: Why was the hospital so noisy?

A: All the sick beats.

299. Q: What did the bed say to the hospital?

A: "I'm occupied."

Houses

300. Q: Why don't houses play cards?

A: Because they're afraid of the deck.

301. Q: What did the house say to the tornado?

A: "You'll blow me away!"

302. Q: Why did the house go to the doctor?

A: It had a window pane.

303. Q: What do you call a nervous house?

A: A wreck.

304. Q: Why don't houses get cold?

A: They have a lot of layers.

305. Q: What did the house wear to the party?

A: Address.

306. Q: Why was the house so smart?

A: It had a lot of stories.

307. Q: What do you call a house that likes to party?

A: A blast.

308. Q: Why did the house go to school?

A: To get smarter.

309. Q: What did the house say when it got hit by the sun?

A: "That's a bright idea!"

Inflation

310. Q: Why did the balloon break up with inflation?

    A: It was getting too big for its britches.

311. Q: What did one inflated balloon say to the other?

    A: "You're full of hot air."

312. Q: Why don't economists play hide and seek?

    A: They can't handle inflation.

313. Q: What did the tire say about inflation?

    A: "It's getting pumped up."

314. Q: Why was the economy so inflated?

    A: It had too much gas.

315. Q: What do you call an inflated ego?

    A: A pumped-up personality.

316. Q: Why did the balloon go to school?

    A: To get more inflated ideas.

317. Q: What did the dollar bill say about inflation?

A: "I'm feeling stretched."

318. Q: Why was the balloon so arrogant?

A: It was inflated with self-importance.

319. Q: Why did the bread rise?

A: Inflation.

Insurance

320. Q: Why did the insurance company work underwater?

A: To cover liquid assets.

321. Q: What did the insurance policy say to the accident?

A: "I've got you covered."

322. Q: Why don't insurance agents play cards?

A: Too many risks.

323. Q: What do you call a melancholy insurance agent?

A: A blue underwriter.

324. Q: Why did the insurance company become a baker?

A: To make dough on the side.

325. Q: What did the insurance agent say to the romantic policy?

A: "You've stolen my liability."

326. Q: Why don't insurance policies work in space?

A: No atmosphere to cover.

327. Q: What did the tornado say to the insurance agent?

A: "I'm a big fan of your coverage."

328. Q: Why don't insurance agents play hide and seek?

A: They always show up in the claims.

329. Q: What do you call an insurance agent who can't choose?

A: An indeci-sure.

Internet

330. Q: What do you call an internet argument between two electricians?

A: A current affair. Shocking, I know!

331. Q: Why did the computer break up with the internet?

A: There was no connection.

332. Q: What did the spider do on the computer?

A: Made a website.

333. Q: Why was the smartphone so dumb?

A: It lost its connection to the internet.

334. Q: What do you call an artistic internet?

A: A web designer.

335. Q: Why was the Wi-Fi at the gym so strong?

A: It had a great bandwidth and always connected with its

core.

336. Q: What did the computer do at the beach?

A: Surfed the internet.

337. Q: Why was the computer scared?

A: It saw a spider on the web.

338. Q: Why did the cat use the internet?

A: To browse for new purr-chases.

339. Q: Why did the email go to therapy?

A: It had too much attachment issues. You know, always clinging to those PDFs and JPEGs.

Lawyers

340. Q: Why did the lawyer become a baker?

A: He wanted to make more dough.

341. Q: Why don't sharks attack lawyers?

A: Professional courtesy.

342. Q: Why did the lawyer wear a jacket to court?

A: It was a suit jacket.

343. Q: What do you call a sleeping lawyer?

A: A snooze attorney.

344. Q: Why are lawyers bad runners?

A: They always pass the bar.

345. Q: Why did the lawyer go to art school?

A: To brush up on his court-drawing skills.

346. **Q: Why was the lawyer a good drummer?**

   A: He knew how to stick to the beat.

347. **Q: How do lawyers say goodbye?**

   A: "I'll be suing you."

348. **Q: What's a lawyer's favorite clothing?**

   A: Lawsuits.

349. **Q: Why did the lawyer study in the library?**

   A: He was booked for the day.

Leaving a job

350. **Q: Why did the employee bring a ladder to work?**

   A: He was getting ready for his next step up.

351. **Q: What did the resigning employee say to his boss?**

   A: "I'm not quitting, I'm going freelance."

352. **Q: Why did the calendar leave its job?**

   A: Its days were numbered.

353. **Q: What did one job say to the other?**

A: "You're working too hard. I'm out!"

354. Q: Why did the computer leave its job?

A: It lost its drive.

355. Q: Why did the broom decide to leave its job?

A: It was swept away by new opportunities.

356. Q: Why did the electrician quit his job?

A: He didn't see a future with current events.

357. Q: Why did the scarecrow leave his job?

A: He felt he wasn't outstanding in his field anymore.

358. Q: What did the resigning cat say?

A: "I think it's time to paws my career."

359. Q: Why did the shoe quit its job?

A: It was tired of being stepped on.

Life

360. Q: Why don't some people trust stairs?

A: They're always up to something in life.

361. I asked the librarian if the library had any books about paranoia. She whispered, "They're right behind you."

362. Q: What did one wall say to the other wall in life?

A: "Meet you at the corner." They're always coming together on things.

363. Q: Why did the tomato turn red?

A: Because it saw the salad dressing in life.

364. Q: What do you call an illegally parked frog?

A: Toad.

365. Q: What did life say to the calendar?

A: "Your days are numbered, buddy." Talk about putting time in its place!

366. Q: Why did life refuse to play cards?

A: It was tired of dealing with everyone's problems. Plus, life's got a terrible poker face.

367. Q: What do you call fake spaghetti?

A: An impasta in life.

368. **Q: Why don't scientists trust atoms?**

A: Because they make up everything in life.

369. **I told my wife she should embrace her mistakes.** She gave me a hug.

Love

370. **Q: Why did the two hurricanes fall in love?**

A: They had a whirlwind romance that just swept them off their feet!

371. **Q: What did the coffee say to the sugar?**

A: "You make life sweeter and I can't espresso my love enough for you."

372. **Q: Why did the phone fall in love?**

A: It couldn't help but make a connection.

373. **Q: What did the stamp say to the envelope?**

A: "I'm stuck on you."

374. **Q: Why did the magnet fall in love?**

A: It couldn't resist the attraction.

375. Q: What did the farmer give his wife for Valentine's Day?

A: Hogs and kisses.

376. Q: Why do skunks love Valentine's Day?

A: They're very scent-imental.

377. Q: What did one volcano say to the other?

A: "I lava you!"

378. Q: Why was the ghost a good lover?

A: He was so boo-tiful.

379. Q: What did the calculator say to the pencil?

A: "You can count on me."

Marriage

380. Q: Why don't some marriages have secrets?

A: Because the husband and wife share the same sentiments.

381. Q: Why did the two pencils get married?

A: Because they were drawn to each other, and their love was always on point!

382. Q: Why did the two volcanoes get married?

A: Because they lava each other.

383. Q: What do you call two spiders who just got married?

A: Web-mates.

384. Q: Why did the broom marry the dustpan?

A: Because they swept each other off their feet.

385. Q: Why did the cell phone marry the charger?

A: They couldn't live without each other.

386. Q: What did the husband corn say to the wife corn?

A: "I'm all ears for you."

387. Q: Why was the computer cold in the marriage?

A: It lost its Windows.

388. Q: Why did the belt marry the tie?

A: They were a perfect match.

389.   Q: What did the stamp say to the envelope?

A: "Stick with me and we'll go places together."

Moms

390.   Q: Why don't moms trust stairs?

A: Because they're always up to something.

391.   Q: What did the baby corn say to the mama corn?

A: "Where's popcorn?"

392.   Q: Why did the mom broom get a good night's sleep?

A: Because she swept well.

393.   Q: What did the digital mom say to the analog kid?

A: "Just watch me."

394.   Q: Why did the mom bring a fork to the garden?

A: She heard it's best to fork-get your troubles and dig

into life.

395.   Q: What do you call a mom who's a fantastic gardener?

A: A mom-bloomer.

396. Q: Why did the mom join the orchestra?

A: Because she's already a pro at conducting household harmony and dealing with the occasional off-note.

397. Q: What did the mom tomato say to the baby tomato?

A: "Catch up!"

398. Q: Why did the mom go to space?

A: To claim more space.

399. Q: What did the mother rope say to her child?

A: "Don't be knotty."

Money

400. Q: Why don't dollar bills make any friends?

A: Because they're always being spent!

401. Q: Why did the penny apply for a job?

A: It wanted to make cents of its life.

402. Q: Why did the man put his money in the blender?

A: He wanted to make some liquid assets.

403. **Q: What's a televangelist's favorite currency?**

A: Pray-pal.

404. **Q: What do you call a wolf who's good with money?**

A: An invest-a-wolf.

405. **Q: Why did the dollar break up with the penny?**

A: It just didn't make cents.

406. **Q: Why did the man put his cash in the freezer?**

A: He wanted cold hard cash.

407. **Q: What do you call a rich fish?**

A: A goldfish.

408. **Q: Why was the belt bankrupt?**

A: It couldn't hold up its pants.

409. **Q: How does the moon make money?**

A: It has a night job.

Mortgages

410. **Q: Why don't mortgages get invited to parties?**

A: They're a real loaner.

411. **Q: What did the mortgage say to the bank?**

A: "You own me."

412. **Q: Why was the mortgage so depressing?**

A: It was a downer.

413. **Q: What do you call an indecisive mortgage?**

A: A maybe-gage.

414. **Q: Why did the mortgage go to a therapist?**

A: It needed help dealing with its "loanliness". You know, it's tough being a loan out there!

415. **Q: Why was the mortgage so happy?**

A: It was interest-free.

416. **Q: What did the mortgage say to the house?**

A: "I've got you covered."

417. **Q: Why was the mortgage afraid of the horror movie?**

A: It didn't want to see any more foreclosure scenes. Too close to home!

418. **Q: What do you call a psychic mortgage?**

A: A foreseen loan.

419. **Q: Why was the mortgage a good comedian?**

A: It knew how to keep the interest rolling and always had a principal joke up its sleeve.

Mothers-in-Law

420. **Q: Why don't mothers-in-law ever use a map?**

A: They never believe there's more than one way to do things.

421. **Q: What do you call a mother-in-law who's a great cook?**

A: A rare medium well done.

422. **Q: Why did the mother-in-law bring a ladder to our house?**

A: She said she wanted to see our family on a higher level.

423. **Q: Why are mothers-in-law like magicians?**

A: Every time they visit, your food disappears!

424.   Q: How many mothers-in-law does it take to change a light bulb?

A: Just one. She holds it up to the socket and waits for the world to revolve around her.

425.   Q: What do you call a mother-in-law who's good at math?

A: A calculator – she always adds her two cents!

426.   Q: What's the difference between a mother-in-law and a jury?

A: A jury might sympathize with you.

427.   Q: Why did the mother-in-law bring a bar of soap to our house?

A: She said she wanted to clean up our act.

428.   Q: What do you call a mother-in-law who loves gardening?

A: A plant manager.

429.   Q: Why don't mothers-in-law ever knock?

A: Because the world's their stage!

Newborns

430. Q: **Why was the newborn artist so good at drawing?**

A: Because it could draw attention.

431. Q: **What did the dad say to the newborn sun?**

A: "You light up my life."

432. Q: **Why don't newborns play cards?**

A: Because they're always a little short on hands.

433. Q: **What do you call a newborn on a beach?**

A: Sandy.

434. Q: **Why was the newborn clock admired?**

A: It had striking features.

435. Q: **What did the parent cloud say to the newborn?**

A: "You're so cirrus!"

436. Q: **Why did the newborn dislike the alphabet?**

A: It always starts with a cry.

437. Q: What do you call a newborn snake?

A: A hiss-tory in the making.

438. Q: Why was the newborn computer so smart?

A: It was born with a lot of data.

439. Q: Why don't newborns follow GPS?

A: They prefer to take the crib route.

Office work

440. Q: Why did the can crusher quit his office job?

A: Because it was soda pressing.

441. Q: What did the paper say to the paperclip?

A: "Thanks for holding it all together."

442. Q: Why don't office jokes work well?

A: They're always a little forced.

443. Q: Why did the computer take a break from the office?

A: To recharge its batteries.

444. Q: Why did the employee bring a ladder to the office?

A: He was climbing the corporate ladder.

445. Q: What do you call a fish who works in an office?

A: An office krill.

446. Q: Why did the office plant go to therapy?

A: It had growing concerns.

447. Q: What did one office pen say to the other?

A: "You're just my type."

448. Q: Why don't office chairs play music?

A: They're afraid of rocking the boat.

449. Q: Why was the stapler sad in the office?

A: Because it always felt attached.

Parenting

450. Q: Why did the baby strawberry cry?

A: His parents were in a jam.

451. **Q: Why don't parents play hide and seek with kids?**

A: Because good luck hiding when you're exhausted.

452. **Q: What did the parent say to the disobedient sun?**

A: "You're grounded!"

453. **Q: Why did the parent bring a ladder to the playground?**

A: To reach new parenting heights.

454. **Q: Why don't parents tell secrets?**

A: Their kids have too many leaks.

455. **Q: What did the diaper say to the baby?**

A: "I've got you covered."

456. **Q: Why was the computer so good at parenting?**

A: It had hard drive and soft skills.

457. **Q: What did the parent corn say to the baby corn?**

A: "Where's popcorn?"

458. **Q: Why did the parent bring a stopwatch to the park?**

A: To keep track of playtime.

459. Q: What do you call a parent who's good at fishing?

A: A reel expert.

Pets

460. Q: Why did the dog sit in the shade?

A: He didn't want to be a hot dog.

461. Q: What do you call a cat who loves to bowl?

A: An alley cat.

462. Q: Why did the cat join the Red Cross?

A: Because it wanted to be a first-aid kit.

463. Q: Why don't dogs make good dancers?

A: Because they have two left feet.

464. Q: What happened when the dog went to the flea circus?

A: He stole the show.

465. Q: Why was the cat sitting on the computer?

A: To keep an eye on the mouse.

466. Q: What do you call a dog magician?

A: A labracadabrador.

467. Q: Why did the fish blush?

A: Because it saw the ocean's bottom.

468. Q: What do you call a cold dog?

A: A pup-sicle.

469. Q: Why did the cat go to medical school?

A: To become a purr-amedic.

Retirement

470. Q: Why did the retiree avoid clocks?

A: He was tired of watching time.

471. Q: What do you call a retired vegetable?

A: A has-bean.

472. Q: Why did the retiree bring a fishing rod to the party?

A: He wanted to catch some fun.

473. Q: What did the retiree say about his recliner?

A: "It's my new office chair."

474. Q: Why don't retirees play hide and seek?

A: Because they don't want to be found working.

475. Q: Why was the retirement party so loud?

A: Because of the oldies but goodies.

476. Q: What do you call a retired computer?

A: An old-timer.

477. Q: Why did the retiree take up baking?

A: To make some dough in retirement.

478. Q: What did the retiree say to the alarm clock?

A: "You're not the boss of me now."

479. Q: Why did the retiree stop watching TV?

A: He had seen all the reruns.

School

480. Q: Why was the belt sent to school?

A: For holding up a pair of pants!

481. **Q: Why did the math book look sad?**

    A: Because it had too many problems.

482. **Q: Why did the student eat his homework?**

    A: Because the teacher said it was a piece of cake.

483. **Q: What do you call a snake who works at a school?**

    A: A boa-tician.

484. **Q: Why was the broom late for school?**

    A: It over-swept.

485. **Q: What did the history book say to the math book?**

    A: "You think you've got problems? I've got too many dates to remember!"

486. **Q: What do school buses and my dad's jokes have in common?**

    A: They're both full of kids!

487. **Q: Why don't you do arithmetic in the jungle?**

A: Because if you add 4+4 you get ate (eight)!

488.   Q: What did the calculator say to the math student?

A: "You can count on me."

489.   Q: Why was the teacher crossed-eyed?

A: Because she couldn't control her pupils!

Sons

490.   Q: Why did the dad make his son learn about electricity?

A: So he'd be shocked at how powerful knowledge is.

491.   Q: What did the dad say to his son who wanted to play hide and seek in the fog?

A: "You mist your chance."

492.   Q: Why did the son bring a ladder to the family game night?

A: He wanted to take his chances to a higher level.

493.   Q: Why did the dad teach his son to be like a clock?

A: So he'd always know his time is valuable.

494.   Q: **What did the dad say to his son who wanted to catch a star?**

A: "Aim high, but watch out for the moon landing."

495.   Q: **Why did the dad ask his son to learn cooking?**

A: So he'd always have a recipe for success.

496.   Q: **What did the dad say to his son who was scared of the dark?**

A: "Don't worry, the sun will rise again."

497.   Q: **Why did the dad give his son a map?**

A: So he'd never lose his way in life.

498.   Q: **What did the dad say to his son who wanted to be a pilot?**

A: "Sky's the limit, but always stay grounded."

499.   Q: **Why did the dad tell his son to be like a puzzle piece?**

A: So he'd always know where he fits.

Sports

500. Q: What's a golfer's favorite letter?

A: Tee.

501. Q: Why did the football coach go to the bank?

A: To get his quarterback.

502. Q: What do you call a pig that does karate?

A: A pork chop.

503. Q: Why are fish never good tennis players?

A: They're afraid of the net.

504. Q: Why did the soccer ball go to the team party?

A: It was kicked around all day.

505. Q: Why did the bicycle fall over?

A: It was two-tired from the race.

506. Q: What do you call a sporty ghost?

A: A team spirit.

507. Q: Why was the baseball team always in trouble?

A: They kept getting caught stealing bases.

508. Q: What's a boxer's favorite part of a joke?

A: The punchline.

509. Q: What do you call an athletic lemon?

A: A sporty citrus.

Summer

510. Q: Why don't oysters donate to charity during summer?

A: Because they are shellfish.

511. Q: What did the pig say on the hot summer day?

A: "I'm bacon out here."

512. Q: Why don't secret agents go to the beach?

A: They don't want to blow their cover.

513. Q: Why do bananas use sunscreen?

A: Because they peel.

514. Q: What did the lake say to the hot summer sun?

A: "Stop beaming on me."

515. Q: What do you call a snowman in July?

A: A puddle.

516. Q: Why did the robot go on summer vacation?

A: To recharge its batteries.

517. Q: What do sheep do on sunny days?

A: Have a baa-baa-que.

518. Q: Why did the teacher jump into the pool?

A: To test the waters.

519. Q: How do you prevent a Summer cold?

A: Catch it in the Winter!

Technology

520. Q: Why was the smartphone wearing glasses?

A: It lost its contacts.

521. Q: What do you call a singing computer?

A: A Dell.

522. Q: Why did the computer go to the doctor?

A: It had a virus.

523. **Q: What's a computer's favorite snack?**

    A: Microchips and salsa.

524. **Q: What do you call an overweight laptop?**

    A: A heavy byte.

525. **Q: How do you catch a tech-savvy fish?**

    A: With phishing bait.

526. **Q: Why did the smartphone go to school?**

    A: To improve its skills in predictive text.

527. **Q: What's a computer's favorite dance?**

    A: The disk-o.

528. **Q: Why don't some websites like spring?**

    A: They get too many bugs.

529. **Q: Why did the computer get glasses?**

    A: To improve its web sight.

Transit

530. Q: Why did the tomato turn red on the subway?

A: Because it saw the salad dressing on the bus.

531. Q: What did the bus say to the car?

A: "You drive me crazy."

532. Q: Why was the train so good at its job?

A: It had a track record.

533. Q: What do you call a sleeping train?

A: A snooze train.

534. Q: Why don't buses play soccer?

A: They're afraid of getting a red card.

535. Q: Why did the bike go to school?

A: To improve its cycle-ology.

536. Q: What do you call a train that sneezes?

A: Achoo-choo train.

537. Q: Why did the traffic light turn red?

A: It saw the bus changing.

538. Q: Why was the subway so clean?

　　A: It always had a good underground reputation.

539. Q: What did the car say to the traffic light?

　　A: "Don't look, I'm changing!"

Trucks

540. Q: Why did the truck stop?

　　A: It got tired.

541. Q: What do you call a truck that tells jokes?

　　A: A funny hauler.

542. Q: How do trucks stay in shape?

　　A: They haul weights.

543. Q: Why was the truck so good at math?

　　A: It was great with haulgebra.

544. Q: What do you call a truck with a sense of humor?

　　A: A jokemobile.

545. Q: Why was the truck so secretive?

A: It was carrying a load of confidential cargo.

546. **Q: What did one truck say to the other at the stoplight?**

   A: "You're haul I ever wanted."

547. **Q: How do trucks stay cool?**

   A: They have lots of fans in the radiator.

548. **Q: Why was the truck so wise?**

   A: It spent a lot of time on the road to enlightenment.

549. **Q: What's a truck's favorite type of music?**

   A: Truck 'n' roll.

Time

550. **Q: Why did the clock get kicked out of the library?**

   A: It tocked too much.

551. **I wanted to learn how to make a sundial,** but I just didn't have the time.

552. **Q: What happens when you argue with a clock?**

A: It's time-consuming.

553. **Q: Why was the calendar afraid?**

    A: Its days were numbered.

554. **Q: What did the digital clock say to the grandfather clock?**

     A: "Look, no hands!"

555. **Q: I used to be a watchmaker. It was a great job, but**

     A: I couldn't find the time.

556. **Q: How do you catch a runaway clock?**

     A: Wind it up.

557. **Q: Why couldn't the bicycle stand up by itself?**

     A: It was two-tired... of running out of time.

558. **Q: Did you hear about the thief who stole a calendar?**

     A: He got twelve months.

559. **Q: What's a clock's favorite spice?**

     A: Thyme.

Underwear

560. Q: Why don't underwear ever tell secrets?

A: They always get exposed.

561. Q: What did one pair of underwear say to the other?

A: "I've seen your dirty side."

562. Q: Why did the underwear go to therapy?

A: It couldn't handle the pressure.

563. Q: Why don't underwear play poker?

A: They always fold.

564. Q: What's an underwear's favorite type of music?

A: Hip-hop.

565. Q: What's an underwear's life motto?

A: "Support, always."

566. Q: Why did the underwear go to space?

A: To become an astro-pants.

567. Q: Why did the underwear break up with the pants?

A: It needed more room to breathe.

568. Q: What's an underwear's favorite day of the week?

A: Wedgie-nesday.

569. Q: Why did the underwear go to the party?

A: To have a tight time.

Winter

570. Q: Why was the snowman looking through the carrots?

A: He was picking his nose.

571. Q: What do you call a snowman with a six-pack?

A: An abdominal snowman.

572. Q: Why was the winter joke book so good?

A: It had a lot of cool jokes.

573. Q: Why did the winter storm go to school?

A: To become a little cooler.

574. Q: What do you call a snowman with a vampire?

A: Frostbite.

575. **Q: What do you get from sitting on the ice too long?**

A: Polaroids.

576. **Q: What's a Christmas tree's favorite candy?**

A: Orna-mints.

577. **Q: What's a snowman's favorite game?**

A: Freeze tag.

578. **Q: What do you call a snowman in July?**

A: A puddle.

579. **Q: How does a snowman lose weight?**

A: He waits for the weather to get warmer.

Wives

580. **Q: Why did the wife sit on the clock?**

A: To be on time for her husband's jokes.

581. **Q: Why don't wives ever tell secrets on a farm?**

A: Because the potatoes have eyes and the corn has ears.

582. **Q: What did the light bulb say to the husband?**

A: "You turn me on."

583.   Q: **Why was the computer's wife so happy?**

   A: Because her husband was a microchip off the old block.

584.   Q: **What did the husband say to his wife on a snowy day?**

   A: "You are snow beautiful."

585.   Q: **Why did the husband watch his wedding video backwards?**

   A: To see his wife back down the aisle.

586.   Q: **Why did the wife go to outer space?**

   A: To find some space away from her husband's dad jokes

587.   Q: **What do you call a wife who makes pottery?**

   A: A clay-mate.

588.   Q: **Why did the wife take a ladder to the bar?**

   A: To reach her husband's high expectations.

589.   Q: **Why don't husbands tell jokes about paper?**

   A: Because they're tearable.

Work

590. Q: What did the lazy ruler say at work?

A: "I just can't measure up to your standards!"

591. Q: Why did the scarecrow become an employee of the month?

A: Because he was outstanding in his field!

592. Q: Why did the boss hire a cat as the new manager?

A: Because he wanted someone who could think outside the box – litter-ally!

593. Q: Why did the office plant go to HR?

A: It wanted to leave, but couldn't find its roots in the company.

594. Q: What did the astronaut say at his job interview?

A: "I need space."

595. Q: Why don't we tell secrets at the construction site?

A: Because walls have ears.

596. Q: Why did the belt get promoted at work?

A: It held everything together.

597. My boss told me to have a good day... so I went home!

598. Q: Why don't some people like their job at the calendar factory?

A: Because they can't take a day off.

599. Q: Why did the computer show up at work late?

A: It had a hard drive.

Workouts

600. Q: Why don't bodybuilders make good comedians?

A: They can't figure out the punch line.

601. Q: What did one dumbbell say to the other?

A: "Looks like we're getting a lift!"

602. Q: Why don't some people do a workout before bed?

A: They don't want to wake up their muscles.

603. Q: What do you call a sheep doing yoga?

A: Baaa-lanced.

604. **Q: Why was the belt so good at the gym?**

A: It pulled everything together.

605. **Q: What did the personal trainer say to the potato?**

A: "Let's get those eyes peeled!"

606. **Q: Why don't eggs work out?**

A: They don't want to get beaten.

607. **Q: What do you call a funny mountain?**

A: Hill-arious.

608. **Q: Why did the bicycle stand up by itself?**

A: It was two-tired to lie down.

609. **Q: What's a boxer's favorite part of a joke?**

A: The punchline.

Zombies

610. **Q: Why don't zombies eat popcorn with their fingers?**

A: They eat the fingers separately.

611. **Q: What did the zombie say to his date?**

A: "I just love a woman with brains."

612. **Q: Why don't zombies play cards?**

A: They always eat the hearts.

613. **Q: What do you call a zombie in a suit?**

A: The Grateful Dead.

614. **Q: Why did the zombie go to school?**

A: He wanted to improve his dead-ucation.

615. **Q: What's a zombie's favorite weather?**

A: Cloudy with a chance of brain

Guide: "Mastering the Art of Dad Jokes"

Introduction

Welcome to the hilarious world of dad jokes, where the puns are plentiful, and the groans are guaranteed! This guide is your ticket to becoming the Sultan of Snickers, the Pharaoh of Fun, and the Wizard of Wit. Dad jokes, a delightful blend of humor and harmless mischief, have stood the test of time, proving that you don't need to be a dad to crack a dad joke.

They're the secret spice in everyday conversations, turning mundane moments into bursts of laughter. Whether you're looking to lighten the mood at the office, bring a smile to family dinner, or just want to keep a few zingers in your back pocket, you're in the right place.

So, buckle up, future comedians, as we embark on this pun-filled journey to mastering the art of dad jokes!

Section 1: Understanding Dad Jokes

Dad jokes are a unique blend of humor that's so bad, it's good. Let's dissect this comedic enigma.

Dad Jokes are the culinary equivalent of a cheese sandwich–simple, a little cheesy, but satisfying. A dad joke is typically a short, pun-based quip that often plays on words or uses a predictable setup and punchline.

These jokes are the Swiss Army knives of humour – versatile, straightforward, and always ready for action. They're known for being punny, often predictable, and delivered with a mischievous grin.

Their harmlessness and simplicity make them universally accessible. Dad jokes are like the comfort food of comedy. They've been passed down through generations, cementing their place in family gatherings, road trips, and even in the workplace. They're not just jokes; they're a bonding tool, a way to lighten the mood and spread smiles.

Understanding dad jokes is to appreciate the joy in their simplicity and the laughter they bring, even if it's accompanied by a collective eye-roll.

Section 2: The Anatomy of a Dad Joke

Dad jokes are like onions; they have layers (and sometimes make you cry, but from laughter!). Let's peel back these layers:

The setup is where you bait your audience. It's like setting a trap, but the only thing you're catching is giggles. Your setup is the foundation, the "once upon a time" of your joke. Keep it simple and relatable.

The heart of every dad joke is the punchline, where the magic happens. This is your "aha!" moment, where you flip the script and turn words on their head. Puns and wordplay reign supreme here. The best punchlines are those that come out of left field, yet land right in the funny zone.

Comedy gold isn't just about what you say; it's also about when you say it. Deliver your punchline with an air of surprise and a dash of delight. Timing is the difference between a chuckle and a full-on belly laugh.

There you have it – the secret recipe for a classic dad joke. Mix these ingredients, and voila, you're the life of the party (or at least the dinner table)!

Section 3: Finding Inspiration

Discovering the muse for your dad jokes is easier than finding a matching sock. Let's embark on this comedic treasure hunt.

Dad jokes are often born from the mundane. Just like finding a lost remote, inspiration can pop up in the least expected places – from a grocery store aisle to the quirks of your pet. Keep your eyes and ears open; life's little oddities are comedic gold.

Got a funny thought or witnessed a humorous incident? Jot it down! Your notes app could be the new breeding ground for your next zinger. Think of it as your joke pantry, always stocked with ingredients for laughter.

Dive into the ocean of classic dad jokes. Books, online forums, or even that one uncle who never runs out of them – they're all wellsprings of inspiration. Study their form, delivery, and how they turn the ordinary into guffaws.

Remember, inspiration for dad jokes is all around – you just need to view the world through your 'pun-tinted' glasses. Happy hunting!

Section 4: Crafting Your Own Dad Jokes

Creating your own dad jokes is like making a sandwich – you've got to layer it right. Here's your recipe for some homemade humor:

The best dad jokes are like a good haircut – short and neat. Choose words that are simple yet ripe for punning. The punch is stronger when the joke is shorter.

Tailor your jokes to your audience or situation. Like a chameleon on a disco ball, your jokes should adapt to their surroundings. Joke about hobbies, jobs, or even the weather – the ordinary is your playground.

Here is a brief Step-by-Step for your reference:
1. Start with a simple, everyday topic.
2. Find a word or concept within that topic to play with.
3. Twist it into a pun or an unexpected interpretation.
4. Deliver it with a dash of confidence and a sprinkle of silliness.

Creating dad jokes is about embracing the fun in the mundane. Remember, the best ingredient is your unique spin on things. So, keep it light, keep it fun, and let the dad jokes roll!

Section 5: Delivery and Timing

Delivering a dad joke is like landing a plane – timing and approach are everything. Here's how to ensure a smooth landing:

Think of yourself as a chef presenting a dish. Serve your joke with enthusiasm and a cheeky smile. Make eye contact – it's like adding seasoning to your joke. And remember, confidence is key, even if your joke is cheesier than a double cheese pizza.

It's all about the 'when'. The best time for a dad joke? Anytime the mood needs a lift. But beware the overcooked joke – too late, and it falls flat; too soon, and it might not be fully appreciated. Like a perfectly timed soufflé, deliver your joke at the right moment for maximum effect.

Just like a DJ reads the crowd, tune into your audience. Are they rolling with laughter or rolling their eyes? Either way, you've got them engaged, and that's half the battle won.

With these tips, you'll be delivering dad jokes that are sure to land – and maybe even get a round of applause (or groans, which are just as good).

Section 6: Practice Makes Perfect

Just like brewing a great cup of coffee, perfecting dad jokes takes practice. Here's how to refine your comedic brew:

Seize every opportunity to drop a dad joke. Family dinners, meetings at work, or waiting in line at the grocery store – these are your stages. Think of life as a sitcom, and you're the charmingly witty character.

Keep a diary of your jokes and the reactions they get. It's like keeping a log of your comedic journey. Note what works and what gets you the eye rolls (which, in the world of dad jokes, are just as valuable as laughs).

Mix it up! Try different styles, play with words, and explore various subjects. It's like being a chef in a joke kitchen – the more ingredients you try, the more flavors you discover.

Remember, the path to becoming a dad joke master is paved with persistence, practice, and a healthy dose of puns. Keep at it, and soon you'll be the one your friends look to when they need a good laugh (or groan).

Section 7: Navigating Different Audiences

Telling a dad joke is like being a DJ at a party – you've got to play the right tunes for your audience. Here's how to spin the deck of humor:

The key is knowing your audience. What makes your kids giggle might get an eye roll from your spouse and a chuckle from your coworker.

It's like fishing – you need the right bait for the right fish. Remember, humor travels differently across cultures. It's like a passport – it needs to be valid in the country you're visiting. Be mindful of differences and aim for jokes that build bridges, not walls.

Your goal is to spread joy, not discomfort. Think of your jokes like hot sauce - a little bit adds flavor, but too much can be overwhelming. Keep it light, fun, and respectful.

Navigating different audiences with dad jokes is an art form. It's about striking a balance between being universally funny and personally charming. With practice, you'll learn to read the room and deliver jokes that hit the sweet spot!

Section 8: Overcoming Joke Flops

Even the best comedians face the occasional tumbleweed moment.

Here's how to bounce back when your dad joke doesn't quite stick the landing:

Think of a joke flop like accidentally wearing socks with sandals - it's not ideal, but it happens. Embrace it with a laugh and a shrug. Self-deprecation can be a great save. Say something like, "Well, that joke just went on a vacation... to a place where laughter doesn't exist!"

Use the flop as a setup for another joke. If your audience didn't bite the first time, reel them back in with a witty remark about the silence. "That joke was so good, it left everyone speechless, huh?"

Every flop is a lesson in disguise, like finding out the hard way that 'no more tears' shampoo doesn't apply to life. Reflect on what didn't

work, tweak your approach, and remember, the next big laugh is just a dad joke away.

In the grand comedy show of life, not every joke lands. But hey, with every misfire, you're one step closer to mastering the art of dad humor!

Section 9: Advanced Dad Joke Techniques

Ready to level up your dad joke game? Here's how to add some extra zing to your zingers:

Engage your audience with a classic call and response. It's like playing catch but with words. Start a joke and let your audience hit the punchline back. It's interactive and gets everyone involved in the fun.

Every dad joke has the potential to be a mini-story. Embellish your jokes with characters, a setting, maybe even a plot twist. It's like turning a quip into a short sitcom episode.

Don't be afraid to mix genres. Combine a dad joke with a knock-knock joke, or maybe even throw in a little physical comedy. It's like being a chef in a humor kitchen - try different ingredients to see what new recipe of laughter you can cook up.

With these advanced techniques, your dad jokes will go from a chuckle to a full-on comedy show. Remember, the key is to have fun and keep your audience guessing what's coming next!

Section 10: Joining the Dad Joke Community

Welcome to the club of chuckles – where puns are the currency, and laughter is the reward!

The internet is swarming with dad joke enthusiasts. It's like a digital comedy club. Join forums or Facebook groups dedicated to dad jokes. It's a great place to share your latest creation, pick up new material, and connect with fellow dad joke connoisseurs.

Check out local comedy clubs or community groups. Some even have open-mic nights where you can test your jokes live. It's like karaoke, but instead of singing, you're delivering punchlines.

The dad joke community is all about sharing. Swap jokes with friends, family, or colleagues. It's like trading cards, but instead of sports stars, you're collecting laughs.

Remember, joining the dad joke community isn't just about telling jokes; it's about building connections, spreading joy, and keeping the timeless tradition of dad humor alive. So, spread those puns and let the groans roll in!

Conclusion

Well, folks, we've reached the end of our dad joke journey, and what a pun-tastic ride it's been.

We've learned that dad jokes are more than just a series of groans and eye rolls. They're a unique blend of simplicity, wit, and good-natured humor. From crafting the perfect one-liner to mastering the art of delivery, we've covered the A to Z of becoming a dad joke aficionado.

Keep honing your craft, because every eye roll is a badge of honor in the world of dad jokes. Remember, practice makes perfect, and every day is an opportunity to spread a little more joy and laughter.

In closing, remember that dad jokes aren't just about making others laugh – they're about creating moments of connection and light-heartedness. So go forth, spread those puns, and remember: in the grand comedy of life, you're the one holding the microphone!

www.ingramcontent.com/pod-product-compliance
Lightning Source LLC
Chambersburg PA
CBHW081337120626
46546CB00011B/3384